Stuck With It, Not In It

Stuck With It, Not In It

Redefining Life with Parkinson's Disease

SUSAN GANGSEI

Sponsored by the
National Parkinson Foundation Minnesota

DEDICATION

*To my husband, who lived with deep grace
and boundless courage.*

CONTENTS

INTRODUCTION

This book started with the words, "What can I do to help?"

I was sitting in the office of Julie Steen, Executive Director of the National Parkinson Foundation Minnesota (NPFM), knowing I wanted to volunteer for something—something small, something fun. I had just finished my book *The Light in the Middle of the Tunnel: Harrowing but Hopeful Stories of Parkinson's Family Caregivers* and had some extra time in my schedule. Little did I know I was about to embark on an unforgettable journey.

Julie asked if I could write some stories for the NPFM website. I would interview people with Parkinson's disease (PD), family members of those living with the illness, volunteers for the NPFM and medical professionals working with PD. "Just help them tell their stories," said Julie.

Each and every person did have a story to tell, and a message to convey. People told stories about the day they received their Parkinson's diagnosis. They told of watching a loved one cope with PD and of the challenge of figuring out how to support them. They told about the gifts they received from giving to the PD community. Those interviews were incredible and an honor to be a part of.

The people in this book would not use the words *heroic* or *courageous* to describe themselves. They would say that they just looked PD in the eye and moved forward. They could have chosen to stay where they were, in denial or anger, but they decided to reject those tempting modes of surrender. In the process they redefined or refocused their lives, and found ways to contribute to those who live with Parkinson's disease.

They were stuck *with* Parkinson's— it was a fact of their lives—but they chose not to be stuck *in* it.

So, the short and sweet stories for a website turned into this book. A book to raise awareness of the people who live with Parkinson's on a daily basis—and a book to celebrate National Parkinson's Month.

New Lives: People with Parkinson's

Whenever the darker side of Parkinson's is too much for me and I need a little lift, I reread this poem by Peter Gall, who has PD and knows how to smile about it—how to smile, that is, about a fall, hip surgery and the side effects of medication.

ZIP GOES MY HIP

I broke my left hip on a clear summer day,
a day when it seemed life was going my way.

Indoors, a smooth carpet and plenty of light,
my wife at the computer, in a Medicare fight.

And I? I was fooling around in the hall,
no cane and no walker in my hands at all.

(Against Parkinson's rules meant to stave off a fall.)

My spirits were high and my gestures were grand—
until—*kapow!—I could not stand.*

I never did grasp the unfolding events
that slammed me to the floor in a pain most intense.

My surgeon inserted three small metal pins
and sent me to rehab to atone for my sins.

The patients in rehab were a wide-varied lot:
vets, surgery patients, some addicts to pot.

At first, I was hoist in a portable cage.
(My dignity suffered at my advanced age.)

The pills that I took gave me hallucinations;
so I took some more meds and got pill-palpitations.

I learned a tough lesson on pride versus hurt;
use your cane or your walker or with *danger* you flirt.

Peter's poem sums up, for me, the spirit that animates the Parkinson's patients I talked to for this book. Feisty, ironic, honest about the trouble and pain the disease brings, but determined to retain their sense of humor, their sense of perspective and their sense of themselves.

The truth is, people who are diagnosed with PD are faced with the challenge of *redefining* themselves. The phrase "person with Parkinson's" becomes part of their identity—whether they like it or not. But this is also the point at which people with PD can take control of how others perceive them and decide to become more than their disease.

There are several threads that run through the stories of people diagnosed with Parkinson's. First, the plans and visions they had for their lives—their career, their relationships, the future—are taken away from them. These losses are fundamental. Their sense of who they are and what they are doing with their lives needs to change. People can stay in denial and pretend they don't have PD, or that the disease will not change their lives. But the people in this book chose, consciously or unconsciously, to move forward into that change.

Everyone who shared their story with me here found a new purpose, or a new way of living out their purpose. And in every case, that purpose had to do with helping others. Mike Justak became an engineer and an entertainer in order to raise awareness of PD. Liz Ogren moved from being an elementary teacher to becoming a motivator and organizer of people with PD, helping to get them out of their "easy chairs" to exercise and be with others. Steve Holker embarked on a new life that he is still discovering, with the help of a team he has built.

Kelly Cargill, who began her adult life as a mother, now helps medical professionals understand how they can aid—rather than confuse and frighten—people who have just been diagnosed with PD. Ruth Lotzer went from being an elementary teacher to being an artist in order to raise money for Parkinson's causes. Cardiologist Ross Collins became a guide for others traveling the PD journey.

The question each person asks is "How do I keep this disease at bay as long as I can?" with a focus on the quality of their lives rather than the number of years they have left. No one in this group showed even a trace of a "poor me" attitude or spent any time complaining about how hard it is to live with Parkinson's. They don't have time for that. They'd rather live in the fullness of life than curl up and wait for the end. In their quest to live full and active lives they embrace exercise and other activities. Many are doing physical things that are brand-new to them.

The redefinition they've undergone has been hard—it takes time and it calls for a deep look inside. Ross, Kelly and the rest don't deny that Parkinson's is hard for them. They simply choose to take control of how they define themselves, how they live their lives and how they interact with others. They make clear statements about who they are and how they want to live out their purpose.

New Relationships: Families of Parkinson's Patients

PD demands a lot from concerned family members as well. A big part of their life shifts to being with, and taking care of, their loved one. The stories in this chapter show how this change has affected several lives, and how, for some of them, caregiving has opened out into a wider world of action and advocacy.

For Justin and Ashley Remus, their passion for dirt-track racing became entwined with their passion to raise awareness of PD in rural areas. Steve Snater traded in the freedom of the single life to care for his father and mother. Judy Figge started a new business that provides specialized care for those with PD. Kelly O'Keefe works hard to give her parents information about PD and emotional support as they grapple with the life changes that the disease brings about. Louisa Voss retired so that she and her husband could travel the world and raise money for Parkinson's causes.

There's another way in which PD changes a family: it alters their relationships and their roles. This is most apparent in the stories of people who have a parent with Parkinson's. Their relationship with their elders turns into a reversal of childhood—their parents become dependent on them. This dependence can take many forms—physical, emotional and financial—and it can call for major psychological adjustments on both sides.

As the wife of someone with PD, I saw my relationship with my husband change radically. We went from being partners, sharing the daily responsibilities of our home and family, to a time when I had to take on all of them, including caring for him. What we did together and what we shared with each other changed. Our relationship, still strong, was redefined in a fundamental way. This redefinition happened bit by bit, slowly moving us toward something new. As this new relationship developed, it was supported by our love for each other—a love that we knew would stay strong and real no matter what shape it took.

New Commitments: Volunteers

Volunteering for the Parkinson's cause is a conscious choice for the people in this book. All of them live very full and busy lives, but they dedicate a great deal of their time and energy to PD and the National Parkinson Foundation Minnesota. Their volunteer work is a statement of what they think is important, for themselves and for others.

The volunteers in this book have been touched by hardship, and for most of them, it involved Parkinson's. The disease that takes so much from their loved one also takes a lot from them. It's an emotional challenge as well as a physical one. But out of those challenges, they find meaning, and draw upon their hard-won compassion to help others. Their time and talents are a gift from the heart. For them, volunteering is a win-win, give-give situation. Nearly every one of them voiced a familiar sentiment: "the more I give, the more I get back."

Volunteering refreshes Ivy Beebe and gives her more energy. Ann Garrity is inspired by the artists, athletes and advocates who live with PD day in and day out. Guam-born Marie Dydasco-Walch connects with, and cares for, the people in a Minnesota day program; it's how she honors her faraway brother, who has PD. Barb Green turns her active volunteer efforts into family affairs. And Paul Blom works closely and intensely with the NPFM to help change the whole landscape of Parkinson's in America.

New Specialties: Health Professionals

The medical professionals in this book didn't start with a focus on PD. They all began with a more general perspective and skill set. Eventually, though, whether prompted by the presence of PD in their families or simply inspired to do something about the disease, they refocused their professional skills on working with people living with Parkinson's.

Rose Wichmann started as physical therapist, helping people recover their capabilities in a hospital. When she was asked to join the PD specialty clinic in that hospital, she never looked back. Ruth Hagenstuen just knew she was a perfect fit for the job of nurse coordinator in a PD clinic.

Mark Austin and Marcia Cotter expanded their businesses to provide residential, community-based housing designed mainly for people with the disease. Dr. Steven Stein was a general neurologist who learned more about PD when he helped his mother-in-law cope with her diagnosis, and now he's on the Medical Board of the NPFM. All these people refocused their professional skills to help their loved ones and many other people.

According to Rose Wichmann, professionals who enter the world of PD either leave soon—or stay a long time. The people in these stories have stayed a long time. Their stories are about a vocation overlapping with an occupation. They have both a professional and a personal commitment to helping people and their families with their skills and training.

It's interesting to note that in every case their approach to Parkinson's changed as they learned and lived the disease's impact on people. They started by asking purely medical questions: What are the symptoms? What can we do to alleviate those symptoms? How can we cure PD? But eventually all of them broadened their perspective and began asking bigger questions: How do we help the PD patient on many different fronts so he or she can have a better quality of life? How do we minister to and support the families? How do we reach out and help more people with more services?

The world is a better place for a person with PD because these professionals refocused their time, their talents and their hearts. Working with Parkinson's is not just a job for them—it's a commitment, a community and a search for possibilities. They changed their lives—and every day they change the lives of people with Parkinson's. They, and everyone else with whom I had the privilege of talking as I put this book together, took up the challenge of a fearsome illness that still has no cure and—as paradoxical as it may sound—the encounter made their lives richer, more spacious and more meaningful.

I.

NEW LIVES

PEOPLE WITH PARKINSON'S
REDEFINE THEMSELVES

I May Be Stuck With It, But I Am Not Stuck In It

Ruth Lotzer's plan for her life fundamentally changed when she was diagnosed with Parkinson's disease (PD) at the age of 42. "'You have Parkinson's.' Those are three words I heard more than ten years ago—three words that were not in my plan, and I am a planner. I plan the plan to plan," said Ruth. "So my first plan after those three words was to pretend I didn't hear those three words. In other words: denial! I thought that if I just ignored those words, PD would go away. That approach did not pan out, and keeping it a secret was causing me a lot of stress. I needed to make a decision whether to keep on denying PD and be a victim of it, or to be a survivor and get on with my life. I chose to be a survivor, and my first step was to go to a support group."

Ruth's first experience with a support group was hard—very hard. "I am going to be honest; my first support group was terrible! It was a big dose of reality when I started to hear how PD affected everyone's life. I cried the entire meeting. But everyone there seemed to understand. I went back the next month and the month after that. Why? Because it was a place where I could talk openly and freely about what was happening to me—and everyone got it because they were experiencing those things too. I felt better and I could feel my stress level go down. But the more I went, the more I noticed that most of the people in the support group were men. They would give away prizes, just because and for no special reasons. I was always the woman winner because I was the only woman."

Ruth is not only a planner; she is a very proactive person. "I knew I couldn't be the only woman in the Twin Cities area with PD. So, thanks to a website called Patients Like Me, I started my quest to find other women with the disease. One woman I met through the website is Susan Hough—we have become friends. She is my age, has two kids a bit older than mine and has had PD as long as I have.

"Ultimately I found four women with PD, and we decided to have our first meeting. It was great and we decided to meet monthly. I sent out reminder emails and Susan Hough found the room. Our group now has over 40 members and we call ourselves the Parkinsisters. Our group continues to grow thanks to people like Joan Hlas, social worker at Struthers Parkinson's Center; Dr. Daniel Kuyper MD, neurologist at Struthers and Park Nicollet Clinic; and Dr. Sotirios Parashos MD PhD, neurologist at Struthers and the Minneapolis Clinic of Neurology, who tell new patients about our group. I usually get three to four enquiries a month about our group. The Parkinsisters are a great group of women—full of energy and life ready to fight PD with all their might.

"Parkinson's also put me on a new career path," said Ruth. "My plan was to be a kindergarten teacher forever! But being a kindergarten teacher is hard for a healthy person, let alone someone with PD. The physical demands, the stress and the effort involved in helping kids meet ever-higher educational goals and test requirements, along with my ever-increasing off-times, depleted the energy I was supposed to have for my family. I found myself having to take more and more time off. So after 27 years of teaching and seven years with PD, I made the decision to leave my dream job and become Super Mom and Wife.

"I cleaned, did laundry, cooked, baked, taxied and mowed. You name it, I did it. And of course, my family loved it! After just one month I knew this was not the job for me. I needed something to release my creative energies. It started with some keys and buttons I had left over from my classroom art projects, some wire from my husband's tool box and some beads from my daughter's arts and crafts box. I made a pin from a key wrapped with a button, wire and some beads—a little piece of art. Then I pinned it on my coat because I thought it was kind of cute. People noticed and commented. In fact one woman asked if I would like to make more and sell them at her craft show. I decided I had nothing to lose. If I sold any, I would donate the money I made to an organization working on Parkinson's. I called my pins Key-Pins. For me they carried the idea of helping find a way to 'unlock' the mysteries of PD and to find a cure for Parkinson's. The first day of the craft show I sold out."

This was the beginning of Ruth's crafting days. "I created other pins without keys and I called these Hope-Pins—expressions of hope for a cure for Parkinson's. I am not sure how many pins I have sold, donated to organizations or given away to individuals, all to increase awareness and money for PD research and care, but it's been a lot. The pins have gone many places—in fact, this last spring one of my Parkinsisters took some of them to Singapore," said Ruth with a big smile.

Crafting has added a sense of peace to Ruth's life. As a teacher she touched a lot of lives and made a difference. Now she is doing the same thing in a different way.

Ruth concluded, "'You have Parkinson's' has changed my life and I try not to focus on what I have lost or what the future might bring. Instead I try to focus on the time at hand and what I can do to make a difference. I am so thankful for all the people who have supported and continue to support me on my PD journey. My dad always said, 'On the road of life you will encounter many potholes, but try not to get stuck in one.' PD is a major pothole in my life. I may be stuck *with it*, but I am not stuck *in* it. I just keep moving down the road and enjoying the ride."

I Wish They Would Have Told Me

Kelly Cargill was diagnosed with Parkinson's disease (PD) a year and a half ago; she wasn't even 50 years old. Looking back, she believes she had PD for five years, but she didn't know it.

Kelly's symptoms started with a tremor in the little finger on her left hand. "Just like Michael J. Fox," Kelly said. "It moved to my ring finger. Then my hand and shoulder started to get stiff and sore. I was tired all the time. I ignored it at first. I thought that it was the result of the high level of stress I was experiencing due to family issues. I finally went to a neurologist.

"Going to the neurologist was an awful experience. The doctor put me through all the physical tests, like having me tap my fingers together and watching me walk down the hallway. At the end of the appointment, the doctor turned to me and said, 'You may have PD. Let me know if there is anything I can do to help you.' That was it. There was no information about what to do next or how I could fight PD. It was like I was being told I was going to die—but not getting any information on when it was going to happen, how it would happen or what it was it going to be like. I didn't know what having PD meant!"

Kelly continued to search for information. She met with another neurologist who specialized in PD. Again the experience was awful. The doctor was abrupt, said Kelly had 'Parkinsonian-like symptoms' and sent her on her way. "I didn't get any more information to answer the question *now what*? I left crying," she said.

Kelly consulted with two more neurologists specializing in PD. "At least these two doctors were nicer. But they did the same tests and said the same thing, 'You have PD-like tremors.'"

At the same time Kelly was doing all that she could to take care of herself and alleviate the symptoms. "I went to the chiropractor, I did light therapy, acupuncture—anything I thought would help the tremors and the stiffness go away. I didn't want to take medication because I didn't want to experience the dyskinesia that the doctors told me I would have as a side effect.

"I am not a person who goes online to find information—but my son is. He researched PD and found out that the stiffness and sore-ness in my muscles were symptoms connected to my PD!" Slowly but surely Kelly found the information she needed to live with PD—from the internet, a TV documentary, nurses, physical therapists and other people with the disease.

"Today I take PD medication. My shoulder is better; my tremors almost go away by the end of the day. I have been told exercise is just as effective as, if not more effective than, taking medication. Every day I do several things, including fast walks, Pilates, Curves, biking and stretching. Every once in a while when I push too hard, I give myself permission to take a day off. I am going to fight this. PD is not going to define me. I am still Kelly.

"What I really needed from the doctors was more, and more useful, information. I needed them to tell me that everyone's PD is different and that I could live a long life with Parkinson's. I needed to know how exercise and medication would help me. I needed to know basic things like not to eat protein when I take my medication. I needed to know where I could find a community of medical professionals that could help me and answer my questions as they came up. I know that this is not an easy thing to deal with—but all those doctors and profession-als could have made it easier for me at the beginning if they had taken the time and made the effort to explain PD—not just tell me I had it.

"Michael J. Fox is my hero. I have heard him speak and I read his book, *Lucky Man: A Memoir*. In the book he told his story and shared important life lessons and insights—live one day at a time, choose happiness, let go of unimportant things.

"The future still scares me from time to time. But I recognize that some good things have come from my PD as well. I go to a Big and Loud exercise class, where we share information and I try to inspire some of the older people with PD to work a little bit harder. My daughter gave a speech at school about how well I am dealing with Parkinson's and how I inspire her to look at life challenges in different and positive ways. I was so proud of her and touched by the wonder-ful things she said. My family and friends have been very supportive; I have gotten closer to some of my family members. My ex-husband has come through with love and support.

"When I feel down, I think about the fact that a higher power is driving this bus, and I get to let go and choose happiness. That puts a smile on my face. That is why I have a smiley face hanging from my car's rear view mirror—just to remind me."

We Need to Be Responsible to Others

Ross Collins, a physician, has an impressive medical pedigree. His great-grandfather, grandfather, father, mother and brother were all physicians, as are his wife, a sister-in-law and a brother-in-law. Ross remembers listening to his father, a medical school professor, practice his lectures on radiation oncology. "I grew up listening to those lectures," he said. "He was an amazing man. He established one of the first hospice care organizations in Texas."

Ross's father developed a Parkinson's-like movement disorder that forced him to retire from medical practice. Ross's mother, who was still practicing medicine at 84, became his father's caregiver. As his father's disability progressed, he still frequently went to his office at the hospice. This allowed his mother, a radiologist, to continue to work while she was my father's caregiver.

Ross, a cardiologist, was diagnosed with Parkinson's disease (PD) six years ago. He first noticed a tremor and weakness on his left side. Recognizing what was happening, he had a complete neurologic evaluation, and voluntarily reported his diagnosis to the state Board of Medical Practice.

His employer, his associates and his neurologist were all supportive. That support allowed Ross to wind down his practice while his peers observed him to make sure that he was still providing high-quality medical care.

"People with PD need to be responsible and limit activities that could harm others," he said. "All people with disabilities owe that to those with whom they work, to the people they serve in their work, and also to their community. This is true for anyone with PD, whether they're a physician, a teacher, a school bus driver, a skilled tradesman, a financial advisor, or a retired person who drives his car on local streets. A lapse in memory, an unexpected movement, or a fleeting disorientation could harm someone else. PD is not a private matter."

But Ross has not "quit." For two years he volunteered at Senior Linkage, a service of the Minnesota Board on Aging that helps seniors, their families and caregivers find the resources they need. Ross helped people understand their Medicare coverage. He also became a member of the patient council at the hospital where he had practiced medicine. He no longer considers himself a physician. He doesn't use the title *Doctor* when he introduces himself and his photo I.D. says *Ross C., Volunteer, not V. Ross Collins, M.D.*

He's active with the National Parkinson Foundation Minnesota and at the Struthers Parkinson's Center in Golden Valley, Minnesota. "I exercise at the Struthers Center, participate in the Foundation's Pedal and Roll events [bike rides and walks for people with Parkinson's and their families and friends] and ski with other Parkinson's patients," he said.

While at Struthers, Ross sometimes encounters people in the lobby or hallway who have a new diagnosis of Parkinson's and are undergoing their initial evaluation. Some of them appear overwhelmed and in distress. "They look like a deer caught in headlights," he said. "They don't know what Parkinson's means or what to do next. They're scared. I try to connect with these people and let them know that others have been on this journey. I tell them I have been there. I encourage them to take advantage of the many activities and support groups available through the Center.

"My life is even better now than before my diagnosis," he continues. "As a physician I was responsible for my patients. As a physician with PD, I was also responsible for monitoring my own abilities with the help of my peers, recognizing my limitations and retiring before my PD compromised my patient care. Today I am not responsible for anyone other than my family and myself. I get to enjoy the sunshine and I get to help others just starting their journey with PD."

I Am New to This

Steve Holker was diagnosed with Parkinson's disease (PD) in 2011 at the age of 62. He has a noticeable tremor in his right hand and arm.

Like many others with PD, Steve noticed some symptoms a long time before getting a definitive diagnosis. "I probably had PD for a year or two prior to my diagnosis, he said. "I had PD-like symptoms, like tremors, that continued to get worse. When I went to my regular doctor in the spring of 2011 for my annual physical, I mentioned the tremors, but the doctor did not seem concerned," said Steve. "By the late summer and early fall my tremors were getting worse, so I made an appointment with a neurologist. He diagnosed my PD, and told me to come back in two months. I was then dismissed.

"I had no idea what it meant to have Parkinson's. My only points of reference were Michael J. Fox and Muhammad Ali, whose battles with PD had been widely publicized. I was angry and scared.

"Later that day I told my wife, and then we told our grown children. I told my siblings two days later, but I didn't tell my mother. She is in her 90's, my father had passed away a few years earlier from Alzheimer's, and I didn't feel like burdening her with another chronic health issue. About two months later I took her to see her doctor. She saw my tremors and knew something was going on. After significant prodding on her part I told her I had PD. She cried, but then she said 'We'll get through this.' She has a lot more strength than I gave her credit for.

"When PD is new, it's difficult. You look for information about what the disease is and what it means. Everything you read says it's a chronic, progressive disease. The information overwhelmed me. It was sad and depressing and it raised my level of anxiety. It scared me more than it helped," Steve said.

Steve has good days and bad days. One day he can have fewer tremors and more energy. The next day his symptoms are worse and the day is harder. "You can never predict what the next day will bring," he said.

"I worked in sales and traveled extensively in the upper Midwest by plane and car. As the disease progressed, it was becoming tough to do my job—I was exhausted all the time. At a crucial meeting where I was negotiating a $25 million contract with one of my largest customers, I was shaking like a leaf and I couldn't maintain my train of thought." Steve had usually been able to control his tremors in other situations, but here it seemed that the stress of the meeting was making his symptoms worse, as often happens with PD. "I just couldn't perform my job in the manner I was accustomed to. It wasn't fair to my employer, and most of all it wasn't fair to me. I decided to tell my company I had PD," said Steve.

"Their response was great. I worked for several months after I told them about my condition, and then in September, 2012, I went on short-term disability. My company not only made sure I received all the benefits I had earned but they flew many of my peers and a number of the senior managers who knew me into Minneapolis to celebrate my 33-year career. I went on long-term disability and applied for Social Security disability in March of 2013.

"I'm new to all of this, but I've assembled a great team around me to help. My wife and I interviewed neurologists until we found one with whom we really connected; he laid everything out for me without me having to ask. (It helped that he and I have the same dry sense of humor.) Also on my team, along with my wife, are my children. My brothers and sisters call all the time to see how things are going and find out whether they can help in any way. Another thing I strongly recommend is to join a support group. I'm glad I did. Everyone talks openly about their PD and it is good to share with others who have the same disease.

"I get scared from time to time about my Parkinson's and what it will bring. But for the most part, I am doing reasonably well. I try to keep myself busy. I walk a lot, do some yoga and work out at the local 'Y' five times a week in addition to Big and Loud therapy, where they show us how to expand our movements and voice so that they are more 'normal'. We're also fortunate to have a number of friends—including some I have known since grade school—with whom we still socialize. If there is one piece of advice I would give to someone with PD, it's to make Parkinson's *part* of your life, not *all* of it.

"PD did change our future plans in several ways. We were thinking about buying a place in Phoenix for the winters, but at the last minute we decided not to go through with it. Something told my wife it wasn't the right thing to do—and she was right. We didn't need to add more change to our lives and we needed to pause and think about the future in a different way.

"I don't know where the future is going to take me, but I am sorting it out piece by piece. I continue to do things I like and I try to stay positive and have sense of humor. I know things will fall into place as I go."

Shining a Light on Parkinson's

If you want to see Parkinson's in a new light you only need to drive by Mike Justak's home in Plymouth, Minnesota. He shines not one light, but more than 50,000 of them. For the holidays his home turns into what he's dubbed "PD Shimmers," a Christmas light show synchronized to music, in order to raise awareness of Parkinson's disease (PD).

This is not a little Christmas display with a few strings of blinking lights and a speaker outside so that you can listen to a Christmas carol or two. PD Shimmers is a synchronized light show of 58,000 lights that encompasses not only Mike's house, but also those of five neighbors. The light show is controlled by a computer that includes wireless technology so that Mike can come out and direct the show from his Wii guitar. There is a tree of lights that towers 17 feet. The music is broadcast in FM stereo so that you can listen to it your car. There are even battery-powered light wands that Mike offers to onlookers so that they can become part of the show.

Mike wasn't always so outgoing about his battle with Parkinson's. He is a young-onset patient, diagnosed in 2004 at the age of 48. Initially he went through several stages of denial and withdrawal, preferring that no one except his immediate family know of his diagnosis. But almost a year and a half later he had what he calls "an awakening," which led him to found his own nonprofit, The Mike Justak Foundation for Parkinson's Disease. Mike's foundation raises awareness of Parkinson's through the light show, videos in which people with early-onset PD tell their stories and an exercise workout that is done with a Nintendo Wii.

In 2010, with no electrical or programming knowledge, Mike decided to put on a light show. "'Shimmers': that seemed to be a good name for it," he said. "The lights suggest the tremors in PD." So, with 8,000 lights, PD Shimmers was born. It grew yearly, from 8,000 to 20,000 to 40,000 lights. In 2013 there were a whopping 58,000 lights on display. These numbers aren't random: they reflect Mike's deep knowledge of PD statistics. In its initial year the show ran every ten minutes and concluded with an announcement that every ten minutes someone is diagnosed with PD. The 20,000 lights stood for the 20,000 Minnesotans who have the disease. And this year it is expected that 58,000 Americans will be diagnosed with Parkinson's. "We will shine one light for each and every person diagnosed," said Mike.

It's been noted by a number of observers that many people with PD choose to develop their creative side. Mike would tend to agree. For over 20 years he worked in the self-storage industry, most recently as an analyst. Now retired due to the effects of his PD, he spends his time perfecting his light show, telling the stories of other people with early-onset PD on his website and creating a video of faces of people of all ages that have PD.

Mike also developed a batch of new skills. He taught himself building, electrical work, plumbing, music and computer programing as he developed Shimmers. He also designed the whole display to be "Parkinson's-friendly," that is, as easy as possible for him to set up. For example, the center pole of the 17-foot-tall Christmas tree is in three telescoping sections so the balance-challenged Justak can stay off a ladder and work on it on the ground.

"The payoff," says Mike, "is when someone shakes my hand to thank me—and then they tell me they have PD."

Though he's best known in the Parkinson's community for his light show, he's equally committed to the work of his foundation. "I use the foundation to educate people about how important exercise is," he said. One tool he advocates is the Nintendo Wii and its Fit workout. "It gets you moving. It can be social, easing depression, and it helps with balance. I'm currently working to expand my involvement with the Wii—I'm soliciting donations of game consoles so I can put them in the hands of those who need them. I hope to expand our Wii grant program so that there are funds available to purchase game consoles so that anyone who needs one can get one."

This spring he hopes to bring his newest project to life. He is creating a video, "Faces of Parkinson's," which he plans to offer to the World Parkinson's Conference and to Parkinson's Action Network to use in their lobbying efforts for more federal funds to fight PD. Currently the funding from the National Institutes of Health for other chronic diseases is significantly higher than for PD. For example, Alzheimer's research is being funded to the tune of $500 million, with $3 billion for AIDs, while PD research receives $154 million. One reason for the gap, say many observers, is that PD has no "face." Most patients are elderly and not socially active, so they're invisible in the wider culture. Mike's video will feature a "wall" of faces identifying themselves and announcing "I have Parkinson's."

"I created the foundation so I could contribute—give back to help others who have PD," said Mike. I'm fortunate. I feel that the question *why me?* has been answered. I was called upon to find ways to use my talents to help others, to inspire and to pay it forward. My lights shine for the world to see. As long as there is Parkinson's tremor, the lights will shimmer."

A Different Path

W hen I was first diagnosed with Parkinson's disease (PD), it felt like a wall appeared," said Liz Ogren. "I was doing what I loved, teaching and raising my kids, and then PD showed up. My energy level, my efficiency at getting things done, my ability to multi-task—all of these started to diminish. Eventually I learned to accept the changes, and to pace myself. I found out that you *can* go forward when you have PD; you just have to go down a different path."

Liz, who taught elementary-school kids for 27 years, had to give up her job, but stays connected with children by working as a volunteer, teaching first-grade readers. "I have found a place where I can use my skills," she said. "The kids don't know what PD is, and it doesn't matter. They just notice that I am wiggly some days, and stiff other days. I hope this teaches them acceptance of the fact that we all have imperfections and challenges, yet we still make important contributions to the world."

A major contribution that Liz has made is the founding of a non-profit to help PD patients. Research has shown that exercise helps diminish Parkinson's symptoms, so Liz got the bright idea of bringing people with PD together to cycle—and Pedal and Roll for Parkinson's was born. Liz's garage is filled with bikes—regular bikes, recumbent (sitting) trikes and side-by-side tandem bikes. She loans them out to people with Parkinson's who want to cycle. She knows that two- or three-wheeling enriches their lives, physically and mentally. "Staying active improves overall quality of life, especially for people with PD," she said. "The idea of Pedal and Roll is to encourage people with PD to get together, enjoy the outdoors and experience the benefits of moving. "I am a motivator," she adds. "People want to be motivated."

Some 180 riders showed up on the first big ride. "I didn't know it then, but this inaugural event was just a peek at what people with PD want and need," said Liz. "Today we bike, walk, snowshoe and spin— and there are still more things that we can do! Our motto is: Movement is Therapy. Staying active improves overall quality of life, especially for people with PD.

"I never expected Pedal and Roll to be such a big part of my life. I don't count the hours I work on it—it's somewhere between five and twenty-five hours a week, depending on the agenda and events. I am always trying to find new exercise options and to get new people involved. When you give to others, it comes back to you."

It's not just exercise that benefits Parkinson's people—it's fellowship; that explains a big part of Pedal and Roll's appeal. "People want opportunities to meet friends," said Liz. "They want a place where symptoms don't have to be hidden or explained.

"That's why I think that every person who is diagnosed with PD should go to a support group. They need to know that PD is a slow process and it is different for everyone. They need to make friends who will be sharing their journey, and see what PD looks like in one year, five years, ten years. They need to know that, while life will be different because of PD, they can still live a relatively normal life for a long time.

"But you have to work at it. When I was first diagnosed, I gave in to the fatigue and the difficulties of moving. The couch became my close friend. My family pulled me out of this rut, and got me exercising. It wasn't easy to get started, but the payoff came quickly. I felt so much better on the days I exercised."

Coping with the changes brought on by PD has also called for some adjustments in attitude. "Sometimes I can't get dressed in the morning and my husband needs to help me," she says. "It feels funny to have my 15-year-old son open up a wine bottle for me. Murphy, my dog, will not leave my side when my dopamine is low. Yet I still clean my house, do dishes, bike, walk Murphy, visit my friends and neighbors.

"I have a bucket list—a bucket list for living, not to prepare for dying. I want to camp overnight at the Tea House at Lake Louise, go back to France and Germany to see the families I lived with in college. I want to bike in Europe. Then I want to learn how to weave and make pottery. My two sons are now teenagers and they are having wonderful experiences that I want to share with them. I have lots to do!"

Liz exudes compassion and acceptance of others who have physical hardships, traits she learned from her mother. "My mother faced serious health challenges and rarely left the house," said Liz. "She always had patience, a warm welcome and compassion for others. I can be there for friends who say 'I need help with my attitude today.' Helping them stay positive helps me, too.

"I can cry, but it's not much fun and it doesn't make me feel better. Being happy is much more fun than being angry. If I can't sleep at night because my meds wore off, I just read a book until my eyes close again. When I'm tired, I take a nap. I get out every day. Some days it's just to the grocery store or for a cup of coffee. I take each day as it comes." Liz feels that she's found a new path that lets her do what she was meant to do—teach and motivate others. "New people and wonderful things have appeared in my life that give me energy and fulfill me," she said. "Good is woven into everything."

II.

NEW
RELATIONSHIPS

FAMILIES OF PARKINSON'S
PATIENTS DISCOVER
UNEXPECTED ROLES

I Can't Think of a Place I'd Rather Be

Life is bittersweet for Steve Snater. He is living with his parents so that he can be a caregiver for his father, who has Parkinson's disease (PD). "It sucks in every way," said Steve. "But it is wonderful that I can be there for him.

"I had the most wonderful parents," he said. "I am an only child. My parents are my number-one role models and I wanted to be just like them. I played a lot of sports growing up, and my dad was at every practice and game. He even drove from Minneapolis down to South Dakota to see my college football games. Things have changed since then. My parents are still wonderful, but today my father has PD and my mother and I are his caregivers."

Steve moved to California after college. On one of his parents' visits in 2004, the family went to see the Queen Mary at its berth in Long Beach. "I could see that something was wrong. My dad was slow, often lagging behind. Two days after my parents got home, they called and told me my father had been diagnosed with PD. Since then he has also had two strokes.

As time went on, Steve could hear more and more weariness and frustration in his mother's voice during those calls home. He vowed to move back to Minneapolis as soon as he could, and in 2007 he did. It was soon clear to him that his parents would need a lot of help. "PD takes a toll on the whole family," Steve said. "Obviously many things have been taken away from my father. He needs help with shaving and getting dressed. He has lost a lot of weight and falls often. Dementia has set in so he has a hard time remembering things, and he can no longer get on the computer to get something done. My mother has a hard time taking care of a 200-pound man when he falls or needs help moving. Some days she's so tired that she doesn't want to get out of bed."

Given the toll the disease was taking on both his parents, Steve decided to move in with them in 2010. "I hadn't lived with them since I was 18," he said. "Deciding, at 33, to move in like that—well, it's been hard. There are some real personal challenges. Going out on dates and having a relationship with someone is tricky. How do I explain why I live with my parents? When do I tell my date about my father? It's hard on the ego. It's also hard to find time to do anything with friends, let alone go out on a date. Some days I have no energy. I have never been a negative person. But sometimes I have to make an effort to see the positive side of things.

"I do have a close group of friends, some of whom have lost their parents. One friend helped take care of his father, who had cancer. He understands what I'm going through. All of them are very supportive; I lean on them when I'm down."

Steve tries to stay active. He played rugby for a couple of years with the Eastside Banshee club in Eagan, Minnesota—"but it's a young person's game," he said. "I love to golf and try to get out several times per week. Actually, that's how I became involved with the National Parkinson Foundation Minnesota (NPFM). I was trying to think how I could help raise money for PD and came up with the idea of organizing a golf tournament. I contacted Luther Amundson and Paul Blom of the NPFM and found out that they have an annual golf tournament to raise money for caregivers' respite care. I've been helping out with that tournament for a year and a half, raising funds through corporate sponsorships from my business contacts. I'm also trying to do more by being on the NPFM board.

"Being involved with NPFM is a great thing. It's self-healing for me. I meet people dealing with the same issues as my family and I don't feel like I am the only one in this situation. Seeing others at the golf tournament is an emotional relief.

"Right now life is bittersweet for me," said Steve. "There are some good things and there are some hard things. But I can't think of a place I'd rather be."

I Am Not Going to Build That Ramp Until I Have To

Louisa Voss and her husband, Gregg, should probably get some kind of award for the most miles traveled since Gregg was diagnosed with Parkinson's disease (PD) in 2006. Gregg grew up on a farm and enjoyed hunting, a passion he still pursues. Since the day of the diagnosis, Louisa and Gregg have been globetrotters. They've gone to Africa to hunt game. This summer Gregg will go to the Deadwood, South Dakota area to hunt prairie dogs; in the fall he's off to New Mexico elk hunting with his son-in-law and grandsons.

"When Gregg was first diagnosed with Parkinson's," said Louisa, "some people told me I needed to build a ramp up to the house right away to prepare for the future. But I'm not going to build that ramp until I have to!"

Gregg worked for a couple of years after the diagnosis. "It was a huge thing for Gregg to retire. I retired early last year as well, and it was an easier transition than I expected it to be. PD makes you sit back and reassess your life plan. You have to live for now."

Louisa reports that Gregg stays active, even when he's at home. And he's still sharp in many areas. "Gregg doesn't shake when he shoots a gun," she said. "He shoots trap and sporting clays and his aim is dead on. Sometimes I hear his gun go off at eleven o'clock at night and I know that he has shot a coyote that he saw out in our field. Gregg put up a new shed and has a huge garden of vegetables and flowers that people want to give me credit for. In some ways he's sharper than I am."

The Vosses, with extended family and friends, have participated in three of the annual Moving Day Twin Cities, a walk for Parkinson's, fundraising events sponsored by the National Parkinson Foundation Minnesota (NPFM). "We are a pretty competitive family, and strive to raise the most money as a team," says Louisa. "This year we raised almost $14,000 between pledges for the walk and our pool tournament."

That pool tournament, by the way, was a Voss family idea, the brainchild of Louisa and Gregg's three children, who are in sales and marketing. "In the two-day tournament, we raised around $10,000," said Louisa. "The next week, I called Julie Steen, Executive Director of the NPFM, and said, 'I'm coming into your office. I have to get all this cash out of the house!'"

Today Gregg still drives, but only locally; Louisa does most of the long-distance driving. Gregg has tremors and his right foot drags. "This is life," said Louisa. "We didn't choose Parkinson's. You can sit back and feel sorry for yourself—or you can keep going on with life. Someday we will probably have that ramp going into the house—but not before we travel some more. And even then, we will keep raising money for the NPFM."

I Learned About Parkinson's Just Like Everyone Else Does

You would think that Judy Figge would have been well prepared to deal with her father's Parkinson's disease (PD)—that she would have had all the information she needed and that she would have known exactly what to do when her father, Bill, was diagnosed. After all, Judy is an RN and owns and operates a home-health company, Prairie River Home Care. Her company provides at-home health care to people with a variety of acute and chronic conditions and operates in 60 of the 87 counties in Minnesota. But Judy said, "I learned about PD just like everyone else, by simply living with it."

Judy first noticed her father's tremors on a family trip to Hawaii. "He was also drooling a bit, but I just thought it was a problem with his teeth," said Judy. "By the next family vacation, one year later, I knew we needed to get things checked out. It was getting worse. I also knew I needed him to move from St. Louis to be closer to me, so that I could be more involved in his care. I moved him to a house near my property."

Bill and his girlfriend, Dolores, moved from St. Louis to Buffalo, Minnesota together. "I loved Dolores and she and my father had a wonderful relationship," Judy said. "But as my father's PD progressed, Dolores' health also declined. She lost the vision in one of her eyes, broke her hip and had cataract surgery, among other things. It was like I was taking care of two kids." On a trip to a local casino with Dolores' son and daughter-in-law, her confusion was clear to everybody. "She would cut up her food and then try to eat off my father's plate with a knife. Dolores' son and daughter-in-law took her back to St. Louis with them. She passed away two years ago.

"I also knew that my dad was not going to last another year in the house. It was time to make another change, and we moved him to an assisted living apartment. This was not a good time for either my father or me. Dad called the place his 'cell.' He did not think he fit in and did not feel comfortable. I didn't trust that he was getting the care he needed, like receiving his medications on time. I sent extra home health aides to his apartment, but it just wasn't working as his Parkinson's progressed."

Clearly things needed to change again. Judy found him a one-level house five minutes from her own home and he now has 24-hour care in place through her home-health company. "I know he would not be alive if he didn't have this level of care," she said. "Thank goodness I can provide it to him."

Today Bill is almost 90 years old. His lively sense of humor runs to bawdy jokes and self-deprecating put-downs. (When asked whether he preferred to be called William or Bill, he responded, "Call me rotten.") "I have heard the same jokes for fifty years," Judy said as she rolled her eyes.

Cognitively, Bill is still present, except when he is tired. He used to be able to walk around the block. Now he can only get to the mailbox and back. "But he doesn't complain," said Judy. "He always said he would rather have PD than Alzheimer's."

"I am just like everyone else," Judy went on. "I had to learn about PD and how it's different from other chronic diseases. I had to figure out what to do each time a change needed to be made. I feel guilty for not spending more time with him and I hate watching him deteriorate bit by bit. The only thing that is different for me is that I can provide 24-hour support to keep him in his home. My goal is to not have to take him to the emergency room or the hospital."

This experience has also led Judy to her next business venture. She and her family have opened Birchwood House, a home in Hutchison, Minnesota for people who have movement disorders like PD, MS, Huntington's and ataxia. "I know that we can offer care in a different and more specialized way, with higher staffing ratios, than a regular care facility," Judy said. "Birchwood is a residential home for eight people and is specially equipped for the needs of people with movement disorders. It was originally built by the Hutchinson's Hospice Foundation. It was perfect for us—and the neighbors. And we have been trained by, and work closely with, the Struthers Parkinson's Center. I didn't know that there were so many people with movement disorders. The only chronic disease that affects more people is Alzheimer's."

Judy's advice to others learning how to live with and manage PD is to "connect with as many resources as you can. Find out what is available and what options you have. And do it early. You know where this chronic disease is going. Don't wait for a crisis, because your options become more limited then. Don't be afraid to ask for help, even when the person with the chronic disease is still in their home. And make decisions as a family—Parkinson's affects everyone."

They Need More than One Another and Me

Kelly O'Keefe's dad was diagnosed with Parkinson's disease (PD) five years ago at the age of 59. "My mom says there were telltale signs much earlier," Kelly said, "but since dad never said anything and he appeared in good health, they were ignored. Even today, dad is still carefree and nonchalant about his PD. If you ask him he claims, 'There isn't anything I can do about it, so why worry or focus on it?'

"Then there is my mom. We talk on the phone every week and she gives me updates on dad. Mom reports all the new things my father used to be able to do and can't do now. It's day-to-day stuff, like buttoning his shirt and putting on his shoes. She has frustrations watching dad change. At first, she said, 'Don't tell anyone, it's nobody's business.' I know my mom needs to share all this with someone, but she needs more than just me to share it with. She needs more help that I can give her."

Kelly's mother has always been a take-charge person. "She can't sit still," said Kelly. "When my parents come over to my house to visit their grandkids, she will start cleaning or working in my garden. She would rearrange my house if I let her. I can only imagine how difficult it is for mom not having control of the situation."

Kelly thinks that her mother is embarrassed by her husband's PD, and struggles with how it limits their interactions with friends. Getting together with family and friends is a big part of the couple's social life, but Kelly's dad can no longer play cards, and her mother doesn't know what to say to friends or how to explain the symptoms of PD.

"My mom says dad doesn't want to go out because of his shaking," explained Kelly. "Dad is uncomfortable with people seeing him eat, too. Plus, now his speech is affected and he is talking less because of it.

"My mom also worries about whether they will have enough money to take care of themselves. She was diagnosed with multiple sclerosis and has had hip replacement surgery, so she has her own pain and other health issues to manage in addition to my dad's PD. They didn't have health insurance when my father had his second heart attack—it was very hard on them financially. I tell my parents that finances should be the least of their worries; taking care of their health is the first priority. But it is hard for them to reach out for help. When I explain programs that provide financial aid, my mom says, 'Other people are worse off than we are. They need the help, not us.' I think their pride and their desire to get through it on their own are great, but they need to recognize they are not alone and help is available."

Despite her insistence on going it alone, Kelly's mother knows that her husband's condition is going to get worse, and she has reached out, at least to Kelly and Kelly's husband. "She may be joking, but she has said that my husband and I should buy their house and move in to take care of them—or put a kitchenette in our basement so they could live with us," said Kelly. "Don't get me wrong—I love my parents; but living with them is not going to work. I watched stress take a toll on both of them as they cared for their own parents till they passed away. I want to do what I can, but even with my two brothers pitching in, we will need more help."

Today PD affects Kelly's father in both hands and both legs, as well as his face. Kelly said, "My dad is pretty laid back about his PD. He's not in denial, but he doesn't want to know much. He says he will deal with each issue as it comes. He even laughs about it. One time when he was eating lunch with my kids, they asked him for more milk. My dad poured them more, spilling it. When my mom told him he shouldn't have done that, he just smiled and said, 'I spilled less milk than *they* would have.' I think his positive attitude about everything will help make his journey easier, but attitude alone will not get him, or my mom, through this.

"The National Parkinson Foundation Minnesota (NPFM) is my go-to place. I get the latest information on PD from their website. I like reading the stories of others dealing with Parkinson's—they tell me I am not alone in this. The information helps me open up conversations with my parents like 'Did you know that voice lessons help people with PD as their voice gets softer?' I can tell them about the resources that they can get at the Struthers Parkinson's Center."

Kelly saw a notice for the Dance to Break a Record event put on by the NPFM—an event to bring people out and show how dance and movement are good for people with PD. "I mentioned it to my parents, expecting them to resist the idea of going," said Kelly. "But they went! They had fun. It was so cute to see them dancing and laughing. It was good to see my mother gather up all the PD material the NPFM had available. It was something I never pictured them ever doing."

Kelly is slowly opening up lines of communication between herself and her parents on the topic of Parkinson's. "We need to talk about what the short term and long term look like, and my parents are beginning to get this," explained Kelly. "What do we need to prepare for, and how we can get help when things change? The information from the NPFM is what we need."

Information—and getting her parents connected with other PD patients—is key in helping Kelly cope with her anxieties about being a caregiver too. "I want to help," she said, "but I'm not sure what to do. I am a good researcher and can look up information and provide links to good websites. I can get them in touch with professionals who can help. But ultimately I don't know what they are going through—especially emotionally. They need to talk to people who understand the PD journey because they have been there.

"I want my parents to enjoy life as best they can while they can still get out and do things. But my mom and dad need more than one another—and me."

They Don't Know What They Don't Know

A shley and Justin Remus live in New Ulm, Minnesota, a farming community about 100 miles southwest of Minneapolis. They're keenly aware of the lack of information and awareness about Parkinson's disease (PD) in small towns and rural areas. In fact, they *lived* this lack when Justin's grandfather was diagnosed with Lewy Body, a movement disorder very similar to PD, in 2007 and passed away in 2011.

"It took three to four years for my grandfather to be properly diagnosed," Justin said. "When our family took him to his primary physician and explained what was going on, the physician believed my grandfather was just showing the normal signs of aging. Ashley and I knew something else was going on. Ashley is an occupational therapist and she knew enough to keep pushing for answers. Once the right information was brought to the physician, he was able to refer us to a neurologist, who gave us the diagnosis of Parkinson's disease. We know that the misdiagnosis wasn't the physician's fault. The lack of awareness of the signs and symptoms of PD makes it difficult for families and doctors to make the correct diagnosis."

Justin was very involved in the care of his grandfather. For a year and a half he lived with his grandparents in order to help out, and when he and Ashley got married, they found a place to live that was only a half-mile away. "My grandfather was a very loving guy," said Justin. "He loved deer and would spend time watching them in the backyard. Sometimes the deer were real, and sometimes they were hallucinations—but it didn't matter. My grandfather also loved Rilee, our yellow lab. Often we would take Rilee to my grandparents so Rilee and my grandfather could just hang out together. When my grandfather was in hospice care, he would always wake up when Rilee came to visit."

Ashley was also very involved in caregiving. During the summer that she was studying occupational therapy in graduate school, she spent many hours working with Justin's grandfather. "I was the only person he would do activities with," she said. "I would give him some exercises to do as 'homework.' He would do his homework for me, but not for anyone else. That summer we became close and I have great memories of that time."

Justin points out that one of the main things that caregivers need when PD strikes is simple, basic knowledge of the disease. "Families have a hard time dealing with the progression of PD symptoms," he said. "It was heartbreaking for me to see my grandfather's decline and not know what to do. Thankfully, I had Ashley to explain the stages of PD and to help me understand its progression.

"Rural areas present additional challenges to diagnosing and living with PD," he adds. "PD can be isolating, but it's even more isolating when you live in the country, far from neighbors. And rural culture can be another roadblock. It's built on being self-sufficient and not wanting to have obligations to anyone. There are additional logistical challenges when you have to drive two hours to see a specialist or to get therapies that can increase the quality of life of those living with Parkinson's."

PD had touched Justin and Ashley's lives even before Justin's grandfather was diagnosed. His great-grandmother had PD and no one knew it—it was diagnosed post-mortem. Ashley's grandfather had PD and passed away when she was nineteen years old. Today Justin and Ashley are touching many others as they work to raise awareness of Parkinson's in rural areas. They help people know what they don't know about PD so people and families living with the disease can get the information and the support they need to live life to its fullest, as long as possible. To this end, they spend a lot of time working with the National Parkinson Foundation Minnesota (NPFM).

Justin drives a modified dirt-track car in races during the summer. His car is covered with NPFM logos and all the proceeds from his sale of tee shirts and sweat shirts go to the foundation. Last summer he raced 59 nights in eight towns in Minnesota. In each city, one night's racing program was dedicated to raising awareness of PD. Ashley and Justin gave out materials on the disease and had a balloon release prior to the night's feature event to honor those who lived, and those who still live, with PD. "I still tear up when I think of all those balloons floating in the sky," said Ashley.

39

Justin connected with more than 50,000 people at those races. "It meant a lot to me," he said, "when a woman came down from the stands and told us that she had just been diagnosed with PD. She said, 'It's good to know people are working on raising awareness.'

"The signs and symptoms of cancer are pretty well known; we need to do more to educate everyone about the signs and symptoms of PD," said Justin. "The sooner someone is diagnosed, the sooner he or she can get help and information, like the importance of exercise and staying active in other ways. It also needs to be shared that once a person is diagnosed with PD, his or her life doesn't end. It's the start of a new journey."

III.

NEW COMMITMENTS

VOLUNTEERS FIND MEANING (AND FUN) IN WORKING FOR THE PARKINSON'S CAUSE

It's a Family Affair

When someone calls the National Parkinson Foundation Minnesota (NPFM), Barb Green is the one who picks up the phone and tries to help the person on the other end, whether it's someone with the disease or a family member of a Parkinson's patient. But that's not all she does in the Parkinson's cause. For 17 years Barb has walked and volunteered at the Moving Day Twin Cities, a walk for Parkinson's sponsored by the NPFM. Barb's first walk was in 1997, when she and her sister signed up together. "It's become a family affair," she said. "Now more than twenty of us volunteer for the event, including my husband, daughters, brothers, sisters-in-law, nieces, nephews and friends."

Barb's father was diagnosed with Parkinson's disease (PD) in 1979 at the age of 48. Barb got a call from her mother telling Barb about the diagnosis. "When I heard this news, the first thing I did was to go back to my apartment to look up Parkinson's in the dictionary," said Barb. "I didn't know anything about PD, but I knew it was bad. The website I visited said PD was a disabling disease and that it would change his life—not for the better. I was in my early twenties. I didn't want to see something bad happen to my father.

"At first we didn't have to think about it, since his symptoms were not that bad. We kept on with our lives, occasionally noticing things like how his arm wouldn't swing and that his walking was different. But by the mid 90s Dad's symptoms had become more pronounced.

"The ups and downs of the disease were hard for my mother. One day he could do the buttons on his shirt, the next day he couldn't."

These are the kinds of hard daily issues that you need to share with other people who understand. "I took my father to a support group at the Parkinson's Center at Methodist Hospital [in St. Louis Park, Minnesota]," said Barb. "After a few meetings, my mother joined us in the support group and they continued to go for many years.

"Years later, Dad loved to go to the day program at Struthers Parkinson's Center, where crafts are among the offerings. His specialty was ceramics, something he had never done before. He made seven ceramic dwarfs. When he passed away in 2005, we all wanted the dwarfs. We wanted to remember our dad and grandpa and his willingness to try things that were new to him."

Barb was close to her father. "He was the fun parent, always fooling around with the kids. He put a pool in the back yard so we could spend a lot of time in it as a family. He was a 'hands on' dad. It was hard to see that change as the disease progressed. But in the early 1990s when I started going to the support group with him, our relationship developed in a different way. It deepened."

Barb's first volunteer position was at the Struthers day program that had meant so much to her father. She said, "There was one woman named Marty who came to the program. She loved to be in the kitchen, so I would help her bake brownies and clean up. I helped people take walks outside if the weather was good and helped people get to their exercise classes. Every Thanksgiving the staff would make a big dinner for the clients and their families. The one thing I had to get used to was feeding people and giving them thickened liquids so they could swallow properly. The hardest thing was to watch them lose their ability to communicate as their voices got softer."

In early 1997 Barb took her father to a NPFM Soiree, a social event where people with PD and their families can go out for dinner and feel "normal," even with their tremors and difficulties eating—since everybody has the same challenges. Night Out is a mini-gala with dinner, music, a silent auction and a medical update. This event was the start of Barb's involvement with the NPFM, then known as the Parkinson Association of Minnesota. Barb and her family volunteered for Moving Day Twin Cities. In 1997 Barb joined the NPFM Board of Directors and served for fourteen years—she has become the unofficial historian of the organization.

Barb's mother passed away early this year from cancer. When asked why she chooses to volunteer to support people with PD rather than cancer patients, she replied, "Everyone knows and understands cancer. Cancer groups have lots of volunteers. But most people don't know about PD or understand it—they think it's just tremors. People don't realize there are non-motor symptoms, such as dementia. PD is misunderstood and underserved." And my mother was very proud of our involvement in the Parkinson's community.

Today Barb works part time for NPFM and continues to volunteer there as well. "The other day a woman who was just diagnosed called to get more information about PD," she said. "A wife who is a caregiver for her husband called to find out where she could get some respite care. I can connect with these people because I have been there. I give them information and suggestions. Sometimes they just need to talk to someone who understands what they are going through.

"The people who are involved with the PD community in various ways are amazing. I see people at events that I have known and worked with for years. It's the people that keep me involved in the PD community. "

Being connected has also been good for Barb's daughters. "Their grandfather always had PD while they were growing up," she said. "They looked beyond his disabilities—and they agree that he was always the fun one. They are very compassionate people because of this experience." Barb and her extended family will continue to participate in Moving Day. And Barb's family of people in the PD community will be there as well.

It's My Way of Taking Care of My Brother

Like so many others, Marie Dydasco-Walch has to watch a loved one's Parkinson's disease (PD) progress from afar. Marie is from the island of Guam and her family still lives there. Her journey with PD began in 1976 when her father passed away from kidney failure. His autopsy revealed PD, although he hadn't been symptomatic at his passing. Between 1976 and 1982, Marie watched her two uncles' lives decline until they too died of PD. It was difficult for her to watch them wither away to skin and bones. And now, Marie's greatest fear growing up—that her brother would contract PD as well—has become a reality.

Marie recognized her brother's symptoms on a trip home to Guam in 2007 while her mom was on her deathbed. He was moving more slowly, with shuffling steps; choking often; and taking a long time to process a thought. In 2011 Marie decided to bring her two children to Guam for a ten-day stay at her brother's home, so the kids could have memories of their uncle to cherish. Marie and the children were able to spend a good deal of time with him, although he had already begun to withdraw; she knew that every moment, whether it was spent laughing or in serious conversation, might be his last.

When Marie and the kids had to leave Guam, goodbyes were particularly difficult, since they were saying a final farewell to the brother and uncle they knew. Later in 2012, after Marie and her children had returned to Minnesota, Marie's brother ended up in the hospital after falling and hitting his head, and the medical professionals there officially diagnosed him with stage four PD. Marie understood that he would never be the same.

Today she struggles with how to help her brother from so far away. She knows he's depressed, but he and his family have accepted the disease and are treating it holistically. He also takes dopamine, a medication for PD, which helps with his tremors and the motor impairment. Her brother, once a bright and successful businessman, is now trapped in a declining body. His family is trying to give him the best quality of life in the moment, and to make the most of what remains of her brother's zest for life. But it's still hard for them to see what's happening to him.

"I know they don't want me to tell them what to do or how to handle things," Marie said. "So, on my weekly calls I suggest options and give a little advice. I talk to his wife about the possibility of using thickened liquids, so that there is less risk of thinner fluids going down into his lungs and causing pneumonia. I suggest that the family allow him plenty of time to mentally process things and to speak, without finishing his sentences for him. I take my time talking to my brother too, even if I can only spend ten minutes with him on the phone. His advice is precious to me and he always worries about my well-being. When I ask him how he is doing, he replies, '*todu mauleg*', which in Chamorro, the Guamanian language, means *all good*. I'm blessed to have him in my life." In July 2014, Marie says, her brother will celebrate another year of life.

Marie volunteers in Club Create, the day program at the Struthers Parkinson's Center in Minnesota, and at the annual Silverstein Community Awards Dinner and Benefit put on by the Park Nicollet Foundation. She's bonded with the Club Create clients. "One time I was gone for three weeks and came back to find out that one of my PD friends had been moved to a nursing facility. I cried. I see wives when they drop off their husbands at Club Create. One gentleman was well established in the medical community. His wife makes sure he is well dressed and looks great; he's still proud of his appearance. I can see that his wife is there for him and will love him no matter what.

"I can't help my brother make it through his PD journey in Guam," said Marie. "But I can help someone here. It's my way of taking care of my brother."

Grandfather Peanut Butter

One of my fondest memories of my grandfather is sitting at the breakfast table eating peanut butter toast with him," said Ann Garrity. "I was three years old and he was in his sixties and had Parkinson's disease (PD). I never knew my grandfather without PD. That's the way he was, with the PD mask and a little drooling."

Emmet Rohan was 67 years old when a heart attack finally claimed him. Emmet, like many people with PD, had other health issues. He had heart disease in addition to PD and died waiting for the *Phil Donahue* show to come on television. An attorney in the small town of Kaukauna, Wisconsin, Emmett was a vibrant man, a former college athlete and an avid Green Bay Packers fan. He was also a terrible driver, even before he got PD. "He would always offer rides to people," Ann recalled. "They always found a reason not to get in the car.

"My grandfather was handsome, charming and funny," she said. "I also remember him as a large, strapping man with broad shoulders and big hands and a generous heart. The last thing he did before he died was to give up his Social Security check to bail someone out of jail. He always wore a white shirt. He would go out with the guys to play golf and drink beer after work."

When PD struck, it "cut him in half," Ann said. "He was very proud and didn't want to be seen as weak or needing help. Having Parkinson's was not consistent with how he viewed himself and his life. He didn't want to admit he had PD and did what he could to stay away from medical professionals. I think he was probably scared and didn't want to deal with what they were telling him."

Life was hard for Ann's grandmother as her husband declined; money was tight and she was under a great deal of stress. But after Ann's grandfather died, her grandmother came into her own. "She was a painter and a writer," said Ann. "She was also very resourceful and didn't spend any time feeling sorry for herself. When friends took a trip to France, my grandmother went to the library and read up on France and cooked French meals. She read a lot. When my grandmother died she was writing a novel and learning Russian."

PD isn't the only disease that has challenged Ann and her family. "I think neurological issues are my family's Achilles heel," she said. "Two of my grandfather's brothers had Alzheimer's. Two of his sisters died of brain tumors. I was diagnosed with multiple sclerosis (MS) three years ago. Most people don't know I have MS. It affects my sight and I can physically tell when I don't take care of myself. Episodes, like vertigo and fatigue, come and go. But I can pretty much carry on the life I want to have."

Today Ann volunteers for the National Parkinson Foundation Minnesota (NPFM) to honor her grandfather. "With my MS, I do live with the 'ghost of Christmas future' hanging around in my mind," she said. "But when I need some encouragement, all I have to do is look at the productive people—the artists, the athletes, the advocates—at an NPFM event. These are people living with the disease day in and day out, with no reprieve and no remission. They're my major inspiration."

"I wasn't scared of my grandfather's PD," said Ann. "I didn't feel sorry for him. I just felt a connection to him. We were kindred spirits. I think about him whenever I eat peanut butter. There are so many times I wish I could be eating breakfast at that table with my grandfather again."

A Greeting Card Plus Rain Equals More than Fifteen Thousand Dollars

Ivy Beebe works part-time selling gifts and cards at Jayne's Hallmark store in Shakopee, Minnesota, and full-time at Allianz Life Insurance Company of North America. Thanks to a chance meeting at the store and an innovative employee-volunteer program at the company, she became a champion fundraiser for PD research and treatment.

One rainy Saturday at Jayne's, a regular customer, Paul Blom, came in wet and muddy. Ivy wondered how Paul got that way, and when she asked him, Paul explained that he was President of the National Parkinson Foundation Minnesota (NPFM) and had just participated in a fund raiser, called the NPFM Moving Day Twin Cities, a walk to raise money for Parkinson's research and programs. Without hesitation, Ivy said, "I would love to get involved with NPFM and volunteer. I may be able to help you raise some money."

Ivy knew that Allianz Life contributes to charities their employees support through its Make a Difference (MAD) Volunteer Project grants. This program allows Allianz Life employees to directly impact the community by organizing a group of fellow employees to volunteer. The company makes a donation to the charity for each employee who volunteers.

Ivy knew that if she could get five coworkers to help at an NFPM event, Allianz Life would contribute $100 per employee. She found eight people willing to help at the NPFM golf event that raises money for respite care for Parkinson's family caregivers. "I just asked my friends to help. I thought I might have to strong-arm them a bit. But it didn't take much to get them to volunteer," said Ivy.

The original eight-person headcount of Allianz Life volunteers has turned into 25 to 30 Allianz employees who volunteer routinely at a variety of NPFM events. They have coordinated mailings, prepped bags for a conference and written dozens of thank-you cards to people who have participated in NPFM events. Each time and for each employee, Allianz Life has donated $100 to the NPFM. In 2013, the total volunteer donation was $14,600. The company has also invited the NPFM to be at the Allianz health fair, to make a presentation to Allianz Life's safety committee members and to participate in the company's annual charity fair. Allianz Life is a Parkinson's-friendly company.

Ivy received Allianz Life's Volunteer of the Quarter award for the second quarter of 2013. The award reads, "Ivy believes in helping others. For several years, she has generously volunteered for a variety of opportunities with the National Parkinson Foundation Minnesota. She donates about 120 hours annually at events such as the group's annual Gold Tournament; Moving Day Twin Cities, a walk for Parkinson's; and Give to the Max day. She also writes dozens of thank-you postcards following the events. And Ivy knows that if one is good, then two is better—she's always recruiting others to become involved and volunteer with her."

"I didn't know whether I was going to get the award," Ivy said. "Other good people were nominated as well. But I called Paul Blom to check if he would be coming to Allianz that day, as I had previously mentioned to him that when a winner is chosen, someone from the volunteer organization is also invited. Paul said he had other plans for the day and wished me luck. I also told him if I ever won the award, I wanted him to be the NPFM person who attended the ceremony, since he was the one who got me started volunteering with NPFM." As things turned out, Paul surprised Ivy and was there to help celebrate her award and accept the $1,000 donation on behalf of Ivy's volunteer efforts for NPFM.

"I have become a contact for PD at Allianz Life and Jayne's Hallmark," said Ivy. "As others become aware of my volunteer efforts with the NPFM, I've been approached by coworkers who have loved ones with PD. A colleague came to me after someone in his family was diagnosed with the disease. He wanted more information about what the diagnosis meant and what PD is like. Another coworker told me that me that her spouse has PD, and she asked for assistance in finding out more about the NPFM.

"I also enjoy talking to the customers and coworkers at Jayne's Hallmark store. I share information with them about upcoming events at which I plan to volunteer. Through these conversations I hope to find more ways to volunteer and to encourage more people to take part in events."

Ivy finds time to do all of this with two jobs, four children and nine grandkids. "It's a hoot to be a volunteer for the NPFM," she said. "I'm most impressed with the NPFM respite care for caregivers, and that's because of my own experience.

"My mom lost her leg when I was two years old. She took care of our home and managed to raise six kids out of a wheelchair. She didn't leave home often. For her, going out meant getting down twenty-two stairs and then feeling self-conscious when people stared at her. When I was old enough to cross the street, one of the things I did to help my mom was the grocery shopping."

When Ivy was 23 years old with a two- and a three-year-old, her first husband had a brain aneurysm and then suffered a massive stroke during surgery. I had to take on all of the responsibilities of raising our children," she said. "Though my husband never lived at home with me again, I would bring him home for weekends. Through this, I had the opportunity to experience what being a full-time caregiver would be like. I have compassion for the caregivers; they need to be strong for themselves and the person they are helping.

"I get a great deal of satisfaction helping people—it's like leaving church on Sunday. I feel refreshed and have more energy. The people I have met volunteering have become friends. It's fun to be with friends—and the more I volunteer the more friends and fun I have."

Ivy's friendship with Paul Blom continues to grow. "Paul gets me to move out of my comfort zone. When he opened up the window for me to volunteer for the NPFM, I was petrified. I hadn't sponsored a MAD Volunteer Project and I didn't know if I could find five people at Allianz Life to share my passion to help with the golf event—but I did." Paul invited her to his Christmas party in 2011, where she met Kevin Burkart, a skydiver who raises money for the Foundation. "This was prior to a snowmobile accident in which Kevin lost the use of one arm," she said. "At the time I had high hopes of going tandem diving with him," Ivy said with a smile. "Maybe I still will, since Kevin did complete a record-breaking 151 one-armed skydives during the Imperfect Jumps for Parkinson's event in June of last year.

"Paul and Kevin are inspirational. My husband and I were Paul's guests at the NPFM Twins baseball game. I usually don't sing, but I joined the group to belt out 'Take Me Out to the Ball Game.' It's amazing the amount of courage that comes from doing things with friends, versus doing them on your own.

"Just think of what has happened because Paul walked in to get a greeting card after the NPFM Moving Day Twin Cities walk and I asked how he got so wet."

Being Part of the Parkinson's Community Shaped the Person I Am Today

Paul Blom's road to the National Parkinson Foundation Minnesota (NPFM) began when he was teenager. He had a paper route and mowed lawns for older people in his neighborhood. One of his customers was a woman named Gladys. "Gladys was amazing," Paul said. "She was born in 1900 and lived in a turn-of-the-century bungalow on an oversized lot. Her husband had died of cancer and Gladys was 82 years old and in need of help around the house.

"She would insist that after I mowed half the lawn I come in to rest and drink a Pepsi. I hated Pepsi, but I would drink it and listen to her stories. She would tell me about the times when she took in laundry and raised chickens to make ends meet. Then I would go out, finish the rest of the lawn, trim the bushes and head back in for an organ recital from Gladys. She had taught herself to play the organ and her signature song was *My Wild Irish Rose*. Over the years I helped Gladys out several times a week with yard work and other tasks.

"Gladys always said she wanted to die in her own home. When her family made the decision to move Gladys to a nursing home, she just gave up. She died very quickly after she moved. I was a pallbearer at her funeral and the organist played *My Wild Irish Rose* from Gladys' sheet music. According to my seventeen-year-old judgment, the move killed her."

Although Paul eventually understood that in some situations it is necessary for people to move to a nursing facility, his experience influenced his decision to open up his own in-home senior care assistance company, Right at Home, based in Bloomington, Minnesota.

"In the early years of Right at Home," said Paul, "I spent more time with clients than I can now. There was one client, Ralph, who had Parkinson's disease (PD). He lived with his son. We would come during the day and hang out with Ralph while his son was at work. It was hard to watch the progression of Ralph's PD, including the loss of his ability to talk clearly. One day he kept saying 'I want my cake'—at least that is what I thought he was saying. Actually Ralph wanted his *cane*. Ralph was respected in his community and was a proud man. I hated to see the deterioration rob him of his dignity."

Twelve years ago Paul was asked to be on the board of the NPFM (then known as the Parkinson Association of Minnesota). "At that time I was already involved as a volunteer with the Alzheimer's Association (AA)," said Paul. "Even though no one in my family had Parkinson's, Alzheimer's or any other neurodegenerative disease, I knew that I needed to work with one of these organizations. I took some time to compare the two diseases and their organizations. The AA had a significant budget and a large staff. NPFM had a budget of barely $40,000 and no employees at all. People I talked to seemed to be more familiar with Alzheimer's and there were a lot of weird perceptions about PD. It became clear to me that I could have a larger impact on the Parkinson's community, and so I chose to become a member of the board of NPFM.

"I am so blessed to be a part of the PD community. I am a very different person than I was 13 years ago. The NPFM has shaped and formed me—it's a big part of my life. People with PD live in the moment—and they have taught me to do that. When you talk to them, you need to take your time and let their brain think and then express itself. I have learned to take my time walking with them—for them, walking is slow and very deliberate. Today I wear no watch. I don't schedule back-to-back meetings if I can avoid it. I want to be fully present for the person I am talking to. I want them to know that they are the most important thing for me at that moment."

In 2008 Paul received the Silverstein Community Service Award from Struthers Parkinson's Center. This award is given annually to individuals who have worked to raise awareness, advance research and improve programs and service for the Parkinson's community in the upper Midwest. In his acceptance speech Paul celebrated the many relationships that have come his way through his Parkinson's work by singing the song "For Good" from the musical *Wicked,* which stars the two witches from *The Wizard of Oz.* The song's lyrics concern how both Wicked Witch of the West Elphaba and Good Witch of the North Glinda have been changed by their friendship with each other. Glinda starts out by saying that, while she doesn't know if it is true that people come into each other's lives for a reason, "I know I'm who I am today because I knew you." Similarly, Elphaba tells Glinda that "whatever way our stories end, I know you have rewritten mine by being my friend."

"I have been on the NPFM Board for nearly 12 years," said Paul, "ten of them as President. It has been exciting and rewarding. I have easily received more than I've given. As I turn over the reins of the NPFM board, I know that it is in good hands and is in a sustainable growth pattern.

"I have been working nationally with National Parkinson Foundation (NPF) as the Chair of the Chapter Advisory Council for the past few years. I look forward to working more closely with NPF at a national level to grow and strengthen the chapter network."

Paul wants to see the NPF in every community in the country, providing information and other forms of support to everyone dealing with PD. "We need to support the Parkinson's specialty clinics that provide multidisciplinary help to support to people with the disease and their families," he said. "Until there's a cure, we need to continue raising more funds and more awareness—so we can provide more ways to enhance the quality of life of those living with PD and those providing care."

IV.

NEW SPECIALTIES

HEALTH PROFESSIONALS TAKE ON
PARKINSON'S AND CHANGE
THEIR OWN LIVES

I Know Why I Get Up in the Morning

"M y company is both a personal and professional thing for me," said Marcia Cotter. "My father-in-law was diagnosed with Parkinson's disease (PD) in 2004, and he passed away in 2013 at the age of 85. His journey with PD is the reason my company specializes in caring for people with this disease."

Marcia was one of her father-in-law's hands-on caregivers. "I spent a lot of time researching resources to support my father- and mother-in-law, and then explaining the unique needs of PD to the people involved," she said. "I was the person who made the decision that my father-in-law needed to move out of his home and into a facility. I was the one whom the nurses called when something happened and decisions needed to be made."

Marcia owns and manages Parkinson's Specialty Care in Golden Valley, Minnesota, which provides in-home health services and community-based residential housing for people who live with PD. "It all came together for me in 2003," Marcia said. "At that time my company was offering in-home health services, and I had decided to expand the company by adding residential housing to home health support. I was also talking to Rose Wichmann, manager of the Struthers Parkinson's Center, about what care my father-in-law needed. During those conversations Rose asked if I would be interested in having my company specialize in serving people with PD. So we started to brainstorm what housing would look like for people with the disease."

It took a couple of years for everything to come together and for Marcia to refocus her company. Today she has up to 36 in-home health clients and six homes, all of which focus on movement disorders. Seventy-five percent of her clients have Parkinson's. "Even though my residential locations look like assisted living facilities to people on the outside, they are different," Marcia said. "We're providing what are essentially private residences with a home health license. It's their home, not a facility.

"Parkinson's is different from other chronic diseases—and even different from other movement disorders too," Marcia explained. "PD symptoms are often treated with medication; those medications are complicated—how you give them, when you give them and how to coordinate their timing with meals. The meds often have side effects; and many times, additional medications are given to treat those side effects as well. It becomes a downward spiral.

"People with PD often have problems swallowing, so that liquids don't always go down the right way. They need tests to determine their ability to swallow and they may need to drink certain kinds of thickened liquids. And, of course, there are changes in walking and behavior, 'good' days and 'bad' days—the list goes on. There are so many variables that need special training to understand. We are constantly training our staff."

Marcia has worked with others to build educational resources for people with PD and their caregivers. She utilizes TULIPS: for Better Parkinsons' Care, a training program developed by Struthers for senior residential facilities. The acronym emphasizes what people with PD need—**T**ime, **U**nderstanding, quality of **L**ife, **I**ncreased awareness, **P**ills on time and **S**upport. She is on two national boards—the American Health Care Association and the National Center for Assisted Living.

Marcia plans to continue focusing on providing specialized care to people with Parkinson's. She would like to open more residential facilities, including one for people with early-onset PD in the Minneapolis–St. Paul area, and homes in South Dakota as well. "The people in South Dakota have nothing like this," she said, "and they have one of the highest incidences of Parkinson's in the country."

Marcia's business model was built on having a majority of private-pay residents, but over time she has taken in more people on public assistance. "It's harder to run a business when the government controls your pricing—at a significantly lower level than private-pay," she said. "But if I didn't do it this way I would not be serving the people who need it. Research shows that people with PD do better in a smaller residential environment, like the homes we offer."

For this sharp and dedicated businesswoman, her business is more than a business, and her job is more than a job. "This is the work I was meant to do," she said. "It feeds my soul and I know why I get up in the morning."

It's Not Just My Job—It's My Community

R ose Wichmann's path to the Struthers Parkinson's Center unfold-
ed one step at a time; at each step she found new ways of support-
ing Parkinson's disease (PD) patients and their families. She began her
journey more than 30 years ago in the physical therapy department
of Methodist Hospital, where a small Parkinson's center did multidisciplinary team assessments of three PD patients each week. All the
physical therapists, nurses and doctors would rotate in and out of the
team, taking turns doing the assessments. One day medical director
Dr. Paul Silverstein asked Rose to consider being the dedicated physical
therapist on the team. This assignment was just one of her responsibilities—she also did home care, hospice and senior programs. But the
new assignment was the beginning of Rose's PD journey.

The Minneapolis PD community and their mission to support patients and their families grew. Rose's commitment and role grew with
them. Grants from the Park Nicollet Foundation, Methodist Hospital
and the Struthers family transformed the part-time PD center at Methodist into a full-time, dedicated facility called the Struthers Parkinson's
Center. Today the Center provides medical care, support groups, clinical research opportunities, education, respite care, social services and
wellness activities to people who have PD and to their care partners.
Struthers is one of 29 National Parkinson Foundation Centers of Excellence in the US and 39 globally. To be a Center of Excellence is no
small thing. Its application process lays out three criteria—the facility
has to have an interdisciplinary team specializing in PD, it has to do
credible research in the field, and it must provide outreach in its des-
ignated area.

Rose is Center Manager for Struthers and is at the heart of the
center's drive to support more PD patients and their families with innovative programs and services. "Struthers is my community," she said.
"Most people come here to work and stay for a long time, which really
benefits patients and their families. After all, this work is not for everyone. Staff who leave after a short time don't always seem as connected
with the PD community or see the same opportunity to serve.

"I love my job," Rose added with a big smile. "It is my passion. I love to work with others on the team, provide leadership and administrative support to the center, write and teach." Over the years Rose has had the opportunity to write publications for the National Parkinson Foundation, the American Parkinson Disease Association and the American Physical Therapy Association. With colleague Dr. Sotirios Parashos she recently co-authored a patient resource book for the American Academy of Neurology called *Navigating Life with Parkinson's Disease.*

She's has been involved in a myriad of Parkinson's educational programs and has traveled locally, regionally and nationally to speak to a variety of groups, including small groups meeting in community centers and church basements. During one of her trips to North Dakota a woman from Crosby (population 1,100) called and urged her to come to the town to meet a group concerned about PD. To Rose's surprise, a group of 110 people gathered to hear her talk and ask her questions. "That's only one example of how big the need is for information and support for those dealing with PD, no matter where you live," she said.

When asked for advice for people who have PD, their families and the professionals who help them, Rose said, "First of all, living well with PD is about much more than medication. Second, the person with PD and their care partner are the decision-makers. We need to provide the right information at the right time, based on what the patients and care partners tell us are their goals and needs. Those things are different for everyone. It may be as simple as how to pick up a wheelchair and get it in the back of a car—or as complicated as getting them connected to multiple resources, financial, legal and medical. We have to ask, listen and offer what is needed.

"One of the gratifying and wonderful things about working here at Struthers is that I get to develop new programs and resources to better address the needs of the PD community. I get to build long-term friendships with the staff, the patients and their families. I even make sure that I occasionally still see PD patients as a physical therapist so I can keep in touch with clients and their challenges. This is where I belong and this is where I need to be."

Think Globally—Act Locally

Ruth Hagestuen began to prepare for her place in the Parkinson's (PD) professional community as a nurse in Madagascar and Bangladesh. There she worked in cross-cultural health care and program development. "In Madagascar I learned to listen carefully to people who had a different perspective on their health in order to partner effectively with them to meet their needs," said Ruth. The result was an innovative community health program for children under five and their mothers that was staffed by Malagasy midwives and health educators. The program was supported by the Malagasy government and global nonprofits and expanded to become national in its scope. "This experience helped prepare me for my work with people who have PD," she said. "I try to listen to the needs of people living with the illness, and work collaboratively to find the most effective ways to respond to identified needs."

After her time in Bangladesh, Ruth returned to the US and enrolled in a Master's of Theology program at Wartburg Seminary in Dubuque, Iowa. "Bangladesh was a very challenging experience for me," said Ruth. "There was incredible poverty and resources for meeting health care and quality of life needs were almost non-existent. I needed some time to reflect on this experience. Also, I have always been interested in studying theology. Wartburg was a great place for doing both of those things."

Ruth's interest in pastoral care led to an assignment in the spiritual care department at Methodist Hospital. One day she was asked to work with a Parkinson's support group. In order to get a better understanding of PD, Ruth asked to go through the all-day patient assessment program at the Methodist Hospital Parkinson's Clinic. "The assessment was done by a multi-disciplinary team," said Ruth. "It was a team-based holistic approach that focused on the comprehensive needs of the person with PD, incorporating the goals he or she had into the recommendations from the team of experts." Six months later she jumped at the chance to become nurse coordinator of the PD clinic at

Methodist Hospital. "I knew the position and the program were a good fit for how I wanted to approach the care of people with PD."

The job as nurse coordinator in the multidisciplinary PD clinic at Methodist evolved to a position as Program Director when the Clinic and Center relocated to become the Struthers Parkinson's Center. Ruth later accepted a position with the National Parkinson Foundation as Vice President and Director of Programs, where she worked with groups and PD Centers of Excellence (see page 61) around the country. Today she is back in Minneapolis working part time at Struthers Parkinson's Center as the Community Relations Partner. She also serves as Chairperson of Health Professionals Special Interest Group of the International Parkinson's and Movement Disorders Society and she continues as Director of Allied Team Training for Parkinson's (ATTP), an inter-professional training program for the National Parkinson Foundation.

International travel is still part of her life today. This year, Ruth is speaking at conferences in places like Australia, the Netherlands and Canada promoting inter-professional care for people with PD. "I am very interested in promoting team care, locally and globally. That's where a multidisciplinary team of medical professionals work together to help a person with PD and his/her family," said Ruth. "This is a different medical model than what is typically done in the US health care system today. Some countries, like the Scandinavian countries and Canada, have a health system that is much more conducive to implementing a team approach."

Ruth has been working on two key projects at Struthers. For one, she interviewed 42 care partners whose loved ones died in the previous two years to see how they viewed their experience with end-of-life-care. She found that many care partners need more case management, especially in times of transition. They look for support and assistance in finding the resources they can access to get them through those difficult times.

The other project is designed to establish a care network between the Struthers Center and residential care facilities that are committed to educating all their staff to provide good care for people with

Parkinson's. "When a PD patient moves into a residential facility, they often lose contact with their neurologist and other PD professionals that they have worked with," Ruth explained. "The staff in many facilities do not understand the needs of people with PD—the timing of medications, the 'on-off' times of the day, the Parkinson's mask, the fact that a soft voice is part of Parkinson's, that people with PD need more time to do things. We work with the care facility to identify 'PD champions' on their staff who are trained as trainers to lead the program and, in turn, train all the staff on how to better care for people with PD."

The program started with six facilities in 2012, and Struthers will add three more in 2013. Ruth said, "We have learned a lot and have been delighted that the program has been more successful than expected. We are becoming better able to recommend facilities to PD families, and to work with interested facilities so people whose lives are affected by PD can get the best care possible."

Ruth loves her work. "Now that I don't have daily administrative responsibilities, I have the opportunity to focus on select projects to address concerns that we have been thinking about over the years. I work collaboratively to establish these programs, which meet identified needs, and I make sure they will continue over time," she said.

Ruth's program development skills have been applied globally, but she still sees the importance of the individual. "Professionals need to have the knowledge of their discipline and of the disease being treated. It is equally important to listen to the experience and concerns of each person," she said. "Everyone is different and you need to help the person you are sitting with live as fully as possible. In order to do this, it is helpful to consider their cultural context and their understanding of their own health. This is one of the lessons I learned in Madagascar."

A Project Close to My Heart

It's interesting to see how Parkinson's disease (PD) can guide the life and career of someone who doesn't have the illness. Mark Austin's father, Bill, was diagnosed with PD when he was 85 years old. As far as anyone knows, Bill was the first one in the family to have PD—so there seems to be no hereditary explanation for why he got it—as is sometimes the case with the disease. "I guess it was just bad luck," Mark said. "My father moved to Minnesota from St. Louis, Missouri when my sister noticed he was having health problems in 2004. She wanted to keep an eye on him and to make sure he was getting the best possible care. That was the beginning of my personal and professional experience with PD."

Today Mark works at the Buffalo, Minnesota-based Prairie River Home Care, a home health company that's a true family business. His sister and brother-in-law own it and his niece and nephew work there as well. Prairie River offers a wide range of services, from skilled care provided by health care professionals like nurses and therapists to help with daily activities, for people with health challenges and families who want to keep their loved one at home. Mark joined the family business in 2006 after working at another home health company.

"I do a lot of financial counseling with people to help them understand what their health care options are," said Mark. "I can help people understand payer programs like the VA, Medicare and various programs offered by the state of Minnesota. I help them access web sites to determine how to pay for health care services. The answers are different for everyone and they can change over time. I can help a family get quality home health help or find a family-oriented care facility too. Because of my father, I can see them as people, not just clients. I am aware that they don't have control over their lives."

Mark has another role in the business as well. He runs Birchwood House, a facility owned by Prairie River that offers specialized care and living support for people with Parkinson's and other movement challenges. Birchwood opened in January 2013. While they were managing their father's care, Mark and his sister, Judy, (see page 32) realized that they wanted to create a facility that would offer people with movement disorders a more homelike environment than most care centers provide. "We could have provided more generalized care, or picked another focus, such as cancer," said Mark. "But we understand the need for this kind of place because our experience with our father."

Birchwood can accommodate eight residents and is staffed 24 hours a day; it has one member for every three patients, and the staff has undergone special training including TULIPS, a program designed by Struthers Parkinson's Center in Golden Valley, Minnesota to help health care professionals better manage cares for people with PD. (See page 59 for more on TULIPS.)

"PD is different from other chronic diseases," said Mark. "For example, the staff needs to understand that even though the brain is telling a person to walk, the muscles are not getting that signal. This results in locked knees and stutter steps—and it just takes longer to start walking. A person with PD can have a hard time processing information and evaluating things. They think that they can go bowling or on a trip, and clearly they can't. People with PD have good days and bad days. Some days they can do something, the next day they can't. This requires understanding, patience and training on the part of staff."

Mark said, "I don't get to see my father more than a couple of times a week, since he is in Buffalo, Minnesota and I live 50 miles away in Crystal. Fortunately, Judy manages most of his care, with the help of the wonderful staff of the Prairie River Home Care branch in Buffalo. But when I do have a chance, I love to visit him in the morning. I like to cook one of his favorite breakfast meals: eggs, corned beef hash and biscuits. I bring him chocolates, and sometimes I stop by the Veterans of Foreign Wars hall and get him creamed beef, military style. He tells me jokes and then gets mad at me when I don't get them. Sometimes we watch football together. I love being with him no matter how he handles his fork."

Every Patient Is a Puzzle and a Person

D r. Steven Stein is connected with Parkinson's disease (PD) both professionally and personally. After medical school at the University of Minnesota in Minneapolis, he did a rotation in neurology at the Mayo Clinic in Jacksonville, Florida—and that's when he knew where he belonged. "What's more fascinating than studying what is going on in the human brain?" he asks. While he was in medical school he also started to date his wife, Lori. "She is gorgeous and I didn't think I had a chance with her," he said. He soon learned otherwise, and he also learned that his wife's mother had been diagnosed with PD when Lori was just 15 years old. She had grown up with PD as part of her life.

After Steve and his wife moved to Jacksonville, his mother-in-law would come to visit them from Minnesota. He took careful note of the PD-related problems she was having, including hallucinations. He consulted frequently about his mother-in-law's medications with Dr. Paul M. Silverstein of the Parkinson's Center at Methodist Hospital in Minnesota. Steven and his wife moved back to Minnesota, in part to spend more time with Lori's mother.

He joined Dr. Silverstein and his partners on the staff of the Methodist Hospital's Parkinson's Center, which later became part of the Struther's Parkinson Center. Today he practices at the Minneapolis Clinic of Neurology and serves on the medical board of the National Parkinson Foundation Minnesota with PD experts from all over the state.

His clinical experience has made him very clear on a few vital points for PD patients. "People with PD need to see a neurologist who specializes in PD," he said. "There has been so much change in the field since I started. We now know that Lewy Body, a Parkinson's-like disease, is not as rare as it was once assumed to be. Medication options continue to change. Everyone with PD is different. They have different symptoms and need a different combination of medications. There can be non-motor symptoms that need to be addressed—mood, memory, constipation, sleep issues and so on. Each person with PD is a unique puzzle and, as a specialist, I try to make all the pieces fit together as best I can."

Steven has ongoing relationships with his patients, seeing them every six months, and sometimes more often. "I also build relationships with the caregiver and the family members," he said. "I look for burnout in the caregiver. It's not unusual for me to see a caregiver come in for the appointment with a smile on his or her face. But when I ask them how they are doing, tears may come to their eyes. An appointment can turn out to be half about the PD patient and half about the caregiver and family. This is very different from what happens in other specialties.

"One of the hardest parts of my job is dealing with the fact that there is no cure on the immediate horizon. We have a much better understanding of PD than we used to. But until we know what causes it, we cannot realistically hope to cure it. We manage the best we can to help people with PD have the best possible quality of life."

ACKNOWLEDGMENTS

This book would not have been possible without the generous souls who were willing to share their stories about living with Parkinson's disease.

Ruth Lotzer

V. Ross Collins

Mike Justak

Steve Snater

Judy Figge

Ashley and Justin Remus

Marie Dydasco-Walch

Ivy Beebe

Marcia Cotter

Ruth Hagestuen

Dr. Steven Stein

Kelly Cargill

Steve Holker

Liz Ogren

Louisa Voss

Kelly O'Keefe

Barb Green

Ann Garrity

Paul Blom

Rose Wichmann

Mark Austin

Julie Steen, Executive Director of the National Parkinson Foundation Minnesota (NPFM), saw the importance of telling stories about facing into and living with Parkinson's. She was the one who started this book by asking me to help people tell their stories for the NPFM website (www.parkinsonmn.org). She was the one who helped these stories turn in to a book to raise awareness of National Parkinson's Month. And she was the one who found these generous people willing to share.

Jon Spayde, my editor, made this book a great book. He understood its heart and soul and made sure those qualities came out on each page and in each story. He was my partner every step of the way, from making sure each story had a clear message to correcting my grammar—which needed a great deal of help.

Laurie Philips, my dear friend, figured out a way to make this book happen. She was my cheerleader along the way. And she gave up family time with Jon, her husband, so that he could work on the book.

Sherry Roberts did a wonderful job of designing *Stuck With It*. She made it something that people want to pick up and read, giving it the same visual energy as my first book, *The Light in the Middle of the Tunnel: Harrowing but Hopeful Stories of Parkinson's Family Caregivers.*

I want to thank the National Parkinson Foundation Minnesota for sponsoring this book and getting it out into the world to those who would benefit from reading it. The foundation is committed to helping people dealing with Parkinson's live full and meaningful lives. What they provide to the PD community is invaluable.

ABOUT THE AUTHOR

Susan Gangsei is an author, speaker, artist and marketing professional. She was also a family caregiver for her husband, who was diagnosed with Parkinson's disease in 2000 and passed away in 2013.

Susan worked in marketing for more than thirty years before writing her first book, *The Light in the Middle of the Tunnel: Harrowing but Hopeful Stories of Parkinson's Family Caregivers*, a "let-others-help-you" book in which caregivers share their distressing, sometimes overwhelming feelings—and their hard-won self-care skills and wisdom.

Today Susan dedicates her skills, experience and time to working with those who live with Parkinson's. She writes about the disease's impact on people and speaks and leads workshops at events and conferences across the country for caregivers and the families of Parkinson's patients.

When no one is looking, Susan slips into her studio to weave. This is a place of renewal and exploration for her. Weaving became her entry point into the art world. "I've found out that I am a creative at heart," she says, "whether it's creating an image that communicates, writing someone's story or doing a workshop that supports family caregivers. The image on the front cover is one of my tapestries. It represents the new path that people living with Parkinson's find when redefining their lives."

Stuck With It But Not In It: Redefining Life with Parkinson's Disease is Susan's second book. She can be reached at Susan@ TheLightintheMiddleoftheTunnel.com.

THE NATIONAL PARKINSON
FOUNDATION MINNESOTA

The mission of the National Parkinson Foundation Minnesota (NPFM) is to improve the lives and the care of families living with Parkinson's disease (PD). It accomplishes this mission in multiple ways.

The NPFM is working to create "Parkinson's-friendly" communities across the Upper Midwest. This is not a brick-and-mortar project, but rather an effort to insure that individuals and families touched by PD have opportunities to be vibrant, engaged members of their communities. The NPFD assesses the readiness of each town or city to serve Parkinson's families. It engages local health care providers to offer quality patient care, as well as exemplary classes and support groups.

The NPFM also meets with local business and community leaders to ensure that the local infrastructure and local events are built and organized with the needs of Parkinson's patients in mind. Today there is a walking path in Willmar behind the medical center that is designed to provide a trail for all people and a therapeutic exercise path for those with PD. In Fargo the wait time for speech therapy was 4 months. Today it is 1 month, the result of speech therapy educational grants the NPFM provided to train more therapists. Currently there are five communities becoming Parkinson's-friendly—Willmar, Alexandria, St. Cloud and Mankato in Minnesota and Fargo in North Dakota.

The NPFM is an invaluable source of information about the disease, provided by Parkinson's experts. It connects people with support-group networks and exercise opportunities in their communities that are familiar with the needs of those with Parkinson's. The NPFM offers family micro-grants to provide respite care for family members caring for people with PD. These grants will soon include companion care to help the caregiver with daily responsibilities, such as grocery shopping, house cleaning, and lawn care, and exercise vouchers for people with PD that are active in multiple types of physical activities.

The NPFM sponsors many events during the year, including Moving Day Twin Cities, a walk for Parkinson's; a golf tournament to raise money for the family micro grant program; Evenings Out, a gala for PD families that includes dinner, a silent auction and an educational component; and Dance to Break a Record, which demonstrates the value of exercise and other kinds of movement for improving the quality of life of people with PD. In 2014 NPF is also sponsoring "Living with Parkinson's", a program on Twin Cities Public Television aimed at educating families about the disease.

Hundreds of volunteers now join the NPFM to provide education, to support events and to deliver programs to help the Parkinson's community. The members of that community—volunteers, staff, patients, caregivers, friends and loved ones—love being involved with the NPFM. Their involvement not only produces tangible results, it helps them express their gratitude to a compassionate and effective organization. These PD fighters have a lot of fun, too, while they dedicate themselves to doing whatever it takes to beat the disease.

Through this work, the NPFM improves lives, increases understanding of Parkinson's disease and shines light on the critical need for community support. "Until there is a cure, we need to continue to raise more funds and awareness—and to provide more support to enhance the quality of life for families living with PD," says Paul Blom, a former president of the NPFM and currently the CEO of Right at Home, a home care service for seniors.

Join this vibrant group of caring people. Go to www.parkinsonmn. org for more information, and to volunteer and donate.

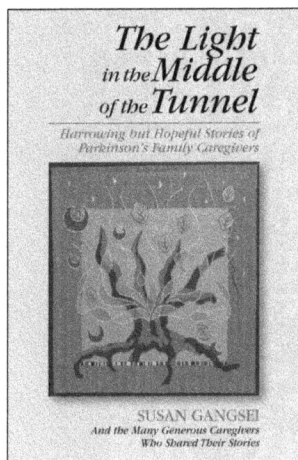

The Light in the Middle of the Tunnel

Harrowing but Hopeful Stories of Parkinson's Family Caregivers

By Susan Gangsei
And the Many Generous Caregivers
Who Shared Their Stories

The Light in the Middle of the Tunnel is not a self-help book. It's a let-others-help-you book, in which caregivers of those with Parkinson's share their distressing, sometimes overwhelming feelings—and their hard-won self-care skills and wisdom. It's a support group between covers, designed to help readers with the hardest part of the caregiving process: dealing with their own emotions.

For more information:
Susan@TheLightintheMiddleoftheTunnel.com

Available in paperback and eBook
at Amazon.com and BarnesandNoble.com

www.ingramcontent.com/pod-product-compliance
Lightning Source LLC
LaVergne TN
LVHW091206080426
835509LV00006B/864